Travelwalk

Cover design and layout by
Tamara Morris
tamorris.design@gmail.com

All photographs by Cary Kamarat.

for Ian

Acknowledgements

I wish to express my appreciation to all those who have given me their stimulating feedback and encouraging reviews. Particular gratitude goes out to my publishing consultants Matt Vossler and Rosa Sophia, to my designer Tamara Morris, and to my technical assistant Michael Carmean, for their extraordinary patience and skill. Thanks also to members of Poets on the Fringe for their ongoing camaraderie and support, and to the Federal Poets who have provided me with so many publishing and performance opportunities. For helping me to build whatever following I might have in the Washington DC area, I would like to thank IOTA Club and Café host Miles Moore, Modern Times Coffeehouse host Maureen Nelson, and Elisenda Sola-Sole at the Kensington Row Bookshop.

Travelwalk
poems and images

by
CARY KAMARAT

Hartley-Wildman Publishing
Washington DC

Library of Congress Control Number: 2014951966
Library of Congress Copyright Registration TXu 1-906-078

ISBN: 978-0-615-94989-5

Journeys light our signal fires—
Travel sends out roiling clouds
to tower and stretch beyond the ether,
reaching for a certain native
joy in every star:

Folkdance streamers soft-connecting
all the swirling worlds of spectrum,
step to gathered step, and leaping
far from where we first shared open
hands, and eyes, and hearts.

CONTENTS

dream catcher, for the seven generations

Old man on the Great Plains,
Once a warrior now a child,
Toys with a willow hoop—
And the Great Teacher Iktomi,
Now the Spider Iktomi,
Approaches with a purpose under Heaven.

And he speaks, as a spider
Might speak who must teach us
About cycles and passings—
From the infant to the child,
To the adult and the elder,
From the elder to the infant, and beyond.

And he fills the willow circle
With his web, spinning words
About good things and bad—
How at each stage of life
There are right paths and wrong,
And a right choice: to follow the Great Spirit.

With your face to the Creator
The web of life will capture
Your good dreams, alone-—
And the evil ones that fall
Can no longer hurt you.
For the children, make good use of your dreams.

the great american peace march

Ice-blue skies above the lawn,
sunwashed hooded mummers dressed
in orange and black, against the cold
the mocking dead stream by.
Barren trees lift sugared storm clouds.
Push and smile! And who's on bullhorn?
Just the press all caged in placards:
HAIRSTYLISTS FOR PEACE AND JUSTICE.
VETERANS FOR ONE MORE CHANCE:
See these boots? inquires the pundit.
*Coulda been your son, these unclaimed
tags*—no smiling glory story:
picture on the coffin, bunting
draped across a roll-roll wagon,
someone sings the red-white-blues.
The President's head in cardboard-mâché
drops away to show the throbbing
oil-drill pulse that drives the brain
inside the blah-blah silhouette.
DC's Finest in their helmets,
star-dash blue and white, at peace
with a rainbow crowd at a bristling barrier:
Gotta give the tourists room!
Gotta gi' duh drummuh some!
High atop the Towering Needle,
Bill and Sally and the children
all the way from West Sandusky,

look down at their favorite view
then askance, at two more hundred
souls awash at the needle base,
sitting, standing, shaping letters:
I – M – P – E – A – C – H.
Whoa! says Billy. *My!* says Sally.
Kids just watch the kite lines twang.
Horses spin to calliope rounds,
jumbling bossa nova beats
from trumpet marchers, tuba dancers
up and down museum steps.
Oil-soaked grassroots press to lobby,
spearhead, coalesce behind
the Lofty Halls of the One Percent
that rule the New Banana Republic—
and yes, we have no, bananas.
But jesters, fresh from writing checks
that roll like tumbleweed across
the lawn, now cry: *Please save our town!*
Evict the Congress, Free DC!
There is another USA:
Thoreau, your boat, so gently down!
And on one park bench,
lonesome, wizened,
camouflaged in shock, one jester
catches a moment's rest, his hand-drawn
placard floating listlessly
above his hunter's cap, proclaims
simply, dryly, only, stop
oh, stop the madness, please.

springsong
for a one-time sleepy southern town

In rainbow shards the lifeblood flows
as love, from heaven to earth.
So quicken hearts and waken flowers,
in seasons of rebirth.

The village has grown, through swamp and pomp,
to Babel soaring proud,
where saplings in the fields of power
might whip and sway, unbowed.

But without children of romance
that rise and learn to sing,
who on earth will ever call
the next and would-be spring?

earbuds

earbuds to keep
the life sound out—
recycled rhythms
canned and stoked
to keep fires burning
gaze hard-fixed
on palm and screen—
she misses eyes
and winks and hugs
still—Solitaire
was good today.

friday night out

he's dressed to kill
she's hot to trot,
they might suck face
but i think not—
no feels to cop
no tickle spot
no longing gazes
love-besot—
but thumbs are busy
tweeting down
my, but don't they
get around.

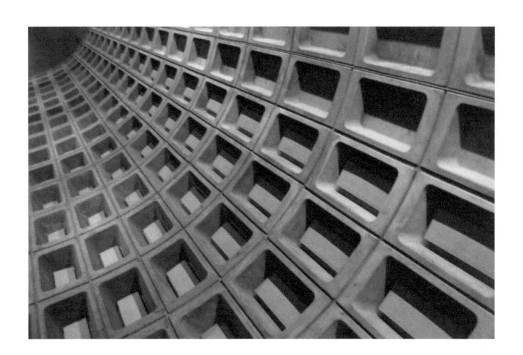

paddleboat dreams

Paddleboat dreams
that ply the golden foam,
keep time, roll on
like softly churning wanderlust,
each turn of the showboat wheel
bathing time in its wake—

From where she watched,
ashore,
her soul awash in memories
she loved but never owned,
the churning silt flowed
past the grand verandas.
A sometime Southern Belle
that somehow never tolled,
she could just see them now,
she could just daydream now,
plantation greens,
and *Scarlett,*
past the elegant lords and ladies
fair and gallant, to each other,
past the levees
where the darkened lives
beneath them sang their pain.

She came down to the river
nursing dreams
little more than the mud
between her toes,
meant to glide a forgiving heart,
stride and rustle
under a broad-brimmed summer hat.

But passion pinched her poetry,
and crinoline was only for verandas
and the prom;
so she wore her plain-weave best,
with baubled gypsy flair
that brought the Middling Sea
far from its home.
She bore her olive foreignness,
among the fair,
among the black,
magnolia sweet and needing
to belong to these, she loved.

Half-porcelain,
on her mother's side,
she never told them of her need
or bought a ticket,
jumped aboard and danced
among the ribboned tambourines.
But she waved, from time to time,
at all the barefoot lads that cried,
Showboat's a-comin'! —
on another shore,
somewhere between heart and mind.

the coyote

The day before you died, a coyote passed
among the dunes,
its tail as fixed and caked
as a Rastafarian's dread.

Above the sequined waves and velvet curls
a daytime moon cried haunting,
ashen and sun-washed,
a turbulence of gulls circled wide.

We walked the tidemark that Sunday morning,
savoring our old age,
and caught the predator's glassy stare
hungering for life, and death.

I thought it was oppressed and beaten down,
I offered doglike gestures
of curiosity and care,
the tilting head, the eyes averted, soft.

It stared unfazed, unswerving
from its purpose, from its hunger.
You never returned to the beach
to feed the hungry beast,
except in laughing spirit, when you came.

long coastal highway

smooth jazz, summernight drive,
whistlin descant, to *easy* jams
my own, Hound-o-Heaven just
ridin shotgun ears *flappin*
howlin judgments like biscuits,
to all them pretty *round turistas,*
smilin grinnin *easy* jazz—listenin,
I just can't handle them biscuits—
all them dawgy judgments just *fline*
right out the summertime winda.

The hound's browns lookin over,
lookin *me* over,
lookin right through me
like he's *trying to eschew me*—

Now *he's* whistlin, bristlin,
joyin the jazz *we are* smooth jazz,
summernight drive,
whistlin descant to *easy* jams
the hound's
smooth
jazz,
summernight drive,
whistlin descant to *easy* jams...

euro jazz at the dragon's cave

Jazzman—steppin out on the
Cobblestones———
Trumpetboy—blowin down from the
Pyrenees—
peakin in at the bars and cafés,
bonin up on that Barce*lona* beat,
goin back to the Renaissance-time———
Harlem, that is
no time for
Shoppin-Across-the-Border,
at your *hy - per - mar - ché,*
we got a scene to make—
Borrachiquitiplím! chiquitiplám!
and it's highly-wired—
funk-inspired but no need to
Wallow-In-The-Stuff
it's only, *Euro Jazz*
at the Dragon's Cave.

Leave your tin box parked———
at a mile high curb———
climb on up to the slum-crumble—
we call, *historic*———
Don't be scared of that medieval vice,
that fall-down look-in-the-sky———
cold stones pushin up
on the wore-down soles
of your dancin shoes———
Just step through that hole
in the crumble façade

let a soft kinda joy—
take away—
the Damp, Night, Chill,
we're movin-on-up
to *Euro Jazz*, at the Dragon's Cave.

Through the billow and grunge——
of a thousand *Gauloises*——
floats a *Ducado* smile—
all rubbery—
and serene——
Mr. Barman'll pour you a fair Spanish measure:
a bucket-or-two——
With Jordi the Music Pimp,
jumpin round in his Big Red Boots——
Two Candy Sweet Lovers press, to the stress brick,
tryin to rub off the blues——
And a Undercover Drag Queen tryin to help out,
be-brandishin her
Mascara Trowel
and the party go *POP! — STOP!*
Everybody go *ss-step and sway*,
cause a four-car Black Locomotive Train-nn
just sent a *Lovin Sound Wave* of *Euro Jazz*—
clear through that Dragon's Cave.

Peakin in at the bars and cafés,
bonin up on that Barce*lona* beat,
goin back to the Renaissance-time——
So Jazzman — Woman — Child...
step up to the Cobblestones.

terra catalana: land of the catalans

By the sea, there flows another sea—
a rising inland stretch of clay and loam
that seems to pitch, and roll, and swell
against a piedmont's rushing mountain shore.

Fruitful now as at the first Creation,
she basks in a sunlit earth perfume,
gracious in the bounty that is hers,
intoxicated, as if with a lover's musk.

Her home is strewn, filled with ancient stones
that dare to nestle, find a broken comfort,
empowered though stricken, tossed and beaten,
bobbing high upon the earthen waves.

And each stone needing to live on
must long for the return, and the refrain—
this sea that is a land will sing their tale,
in the tones of an earthbound sailor's chantey:

> *Song of troubadours once lost*
> *among the smoking battlegrounds*
> *Song of paramours betrayed*
> *offered up to the Black Madonna*

Here the cult of Mary softens the reaper's scythe
and tempers the harvest sickle in its gathering.
Here the keeper's legs, the tiller's soul,
well anchored in the clay,
suffer the ebbs and flows of time and meaning,
lest *politicos* and demigods
carry the tide of history away.

mare nostrum

We've known this sea of ours,
its own reality floating by—
we've slept, and then awakened
to each other's secret gales,

wielding ocean-swords against
immortal powers of stone
that dared contain us,
and her, our precious sea.

Blinded by the dark in tide-swept caves,
we named our grief a somber grotto—
no one's ever come to free us,
no one's ever dreamed a need to be free.

I remember how she preened herself
with devilish pride—like you,
she seemed at quiet odds
with terraces and wicker chairs.

She sang in furrowed cadences,
in waves that climbed umbrella pines
and carried us to the sun,
she shared the wine.

We shared the wine,
and joined her lifting harrowed arms
to battle with the clouds,
to quarrel with our fate—this sea of ours.

flooded mountains

These balmy islands, graced with mai-tai kisses,
black pearls on a bed of watery gems,
with sundown drinks and rainbow toy umbrellas

served up as palm-fronds rustle, slap, and nod—
as gentle waves smooth the rough-hewn edges
of our own exotic seashell picture frames—

these flooded peaks, where the sea has borne us up
to mountaintops we call our sunbathed isles,
are joined together, one beneath the surface.

Beyond our promenades and scheduled tours,
and ferryboat delays that muddle truth
or clouds that darken more than perfect skies,

we are children of these islands, more than not.

queen mary,
and the african queens

Mary, Queen of the Africans,
and of the African Queens,
served others far less masterly—
yet masters, by their means.

She bore her wicker-load with pride
among the grand elite,
through cotton fields and crackling stalks
that made the island sweet.

Cane juice ladled at the boiling bench,
the copper still's kill-devil rum,
King Cotton, mahogany, slaves off the block
made landlords rich as they come.

But Mary, Queen of the Africans,
tended her parchment of land
in the slow time—up to the harvest crush
of souls, and backs, and hands.

*

Awakening dawn, the overseer's call,
first light to the livestock and fields,
and the spirit of Nzinga, the leopard-skinned queen,
hovered over each morning meal.

Nighttime tales of Queen Nanny, of the runaway free,
Maroon towns in the proud leeward sun—
New World colonies of Ashanti on the forested slopes:
Kojo Town, Women's Town, Accompong.

Mary listened and learned, kept the Old Ways with love,
shared the magic of the bold *Orisha*.
So they called her Queen Mary who kept all safe from harm
in the light, and the dark— *Obeah*.

But the Slave Code was harsh, cut limbs and strung necks
in a time of rebellion and fear.
Moko Jumbi went mad in the days of the drought,
madder still in the hurricane year.

*

'Til sultry with sleep, one tropical night,
palms tempted the moon to sway
as jasmine fell softly on lovers' dreams
bathed warm in the ocean spray.

Hammock-strung, the shoreline beckoned
to faithful trade winds from the east:
Come ply the lanes with China rose,
Come soothe the merchant fleet.

But there came a sudden and early dawn—
three torches scored the night,
then ten, and tens, and hundreds more
joined the pooling light.

Three Queens led a rancorous tide enslaved
that engulfed the governor's halls;
and each torch singed its shadows high
upon those hallowed walls.

*

They swarmed along the steps to power,
a buffetted, maddening throng,
to the towering door and the governor standing
agape, sensing reason and wrong.

Clinging now to his old ship of state
adrift on a starboard list,
the grand lord felt all common sense
and the balance of power shift

as Queen Mary softened her lips to speak,
eyes blazing, now bitter, now smiling:
You gon free all de Africa people dem,
or we gon burn every stick on dis islan'.

And so Mary, and Agnes, and *Ma-til-da,*
all queens among African Queens,
brought masters to task on the isle of *Ay-Ay,*
by the wisest and best of their means.

past the prime

Somewhere along the meridian
they looked out over the bay,
past the camel-hump islands
layered to the break,
past the banking mist
that opened to the gentle beast
of the lake. They watched for a sign—
a setting sun sharp enough
to pierce the muddled crust
of cloud and the day's disappointments,
or a mute volcano far enough
around the back of the planet's horizon
to make harmless history of fire.

Even pretty in the half-light, isn't it—
she said, and poured the sounds
into his bone china cup,
lacing the campfire coffee
with interest and hope.
Even pretty in the half-light—
she pressed, cuing the litany,
flicking heels and windmills
at his measured, dying tango.

Yes, I love you—he replied;
and the rusting blaze
of a world-weary sun
broke through at last.

roma

Neglected corners are a haven
from the great encroaching din,
in morning gardens groomed
and tidied for the guest.
These corners,
where salvaged dreams alight on lives
that quicken in a moment's passion—
like lights that wend along a hillside,
like torches that ascend to a lost horizon
these corners make a paradise of their own.

To this neglected garden
the cat will come to yowl,
and thrash at wanton nights—
on hardened paws
the lacerated dawn slinks home
for one last kiss.

Down the street yet far
below the ancient wall
are hidden rooms that love oblivion,
as much as the human shadows that seduce them,
timeless in yesterday's and tomorrow's
smouldering forge.

We feel the fiery stare,
the dwelling glance at every turn,
the deep and passing eyes that swallow beauty—
to recreate, in living portrait, the marble flesh reborn,
in the colorplay beneath the stained-glass rose.

livia

Dear Livia and her brooding seed
preside from high atop the lush
abiding Palatine, where Caesars
dwell, well scrubbed, washed out.
Along one ancient and collective
Roman nose, they all smile down.

Time echoes of the lusty devils,
dust devils funnel upward
off the chariot track that lines
the Circus Maximus, and leave
quite another seed in manly
furrows on the gravelly course.

Dear Livia, out of time
but never extemporaneous,
you tried to teach them how to sing,
how to scheme, and murder and sing,

when all they wanted was a vulgate chant,
to recall you here beyond the rising
river bank, where lovers rant:

ma che caldo	whadya mean hot
qui non fa caldo	this ain't hot
io lo voglio ancora piu' caldo	I like it even hotter
ma che caldo	whadya mean hot

But if remembrance is a kind of love,
they still may love you, Livia Divine,
in a more seasoned, *stagionato,*
more warmly Catholic way.

And no one could love you more than I,
you and all your brooding,
you and all your brood—
unless it be the cat which,
in its turn, is loved.

feline colony no. 3

The Municipality of Florence, Office of Animal Rights under Article Six Thirty-Eight of the Penal Code, serving as Guardian Angel to protect all our Colonies of the Feline Faith, declares to all those who would do Tribal Harm to the Cats that reside here: Mistreatment of Animals carries a Penalty of up to Four Years Imprisonment—

Through the barrier fence, the calligrapher's sign
glistened with promise for a clutter of cats
that shadowed the lane swooping down to the river,
from Piazzale Michelangelo, guarded by night.
Cats about town and elsewhere in the land
crept like the jungle primeval in grace,
purred at their pleasure, or yowled at their passion,
then stalked on, often happy,
just to be.

And a Florentine actress, in baubles and gold
and mascara, heard a tourist all smiles and agleam:

*—I have never in my life seen so many cats
walking free, whatever could they mean?*

Said the thespian, *—You know: Children will
adore us, or fear us, ignore us, and some of
us love them, and some of us hate them,
deplore them, berate them, they may smell
of disease but essentially they're a flourish in
the stamp of creation, and walk on, often
happy, just to be.*

—Children, yes, but the cats?

*—You know: Cats will adore us, or fear us,
ignore us, and some of us love them, and
some of us hate them, and some just
deplore them while others berate them, they
may smell of disease, but essentially they're
a flourish in the stamp of creation, and
they're here in an absence of rats. And
when I'm abroad, my, how I miss them.*
Strano però—*how strange—ma signore,
Where, Are, Your, Cats?*

*—Well, we keep some indoors,
but mostly, we kill them.*

*—But, your children you won't,
I mean you don't...*

*—Oh no we wouldn't,
I mean I'm quite sure we couldn't.
Just the cats.*

for robbie burns

Lusty lads and stronger lassies
Seldom climb the bonnie brae,
Looking down at vales and memories
Thru the lining in the grey.
To shopping malls and welcome cups
They're likely to be drawn,
With a passion just to make it through,
Smiles breaking with the dawn.
Proletarian-lovely Scheme Birds
Twitter in the night,
And the glory of the Bard
Still teaches all to make things right.
When lusty lads and stronger lassies
Remember to climb the brae,
Naught will stop the proud green hills
From echoing Scots Wha Hae.

me familiar
For the Witch of St. Buryan

I wanted to be a witch—a male witch—
but they said there's no such thing
it's not like a male nurse
I'd have to settle for wizardy warlock
and it's not the same, is it—still,
I've got a familiar. He's me dog.
Well he's not *rea*-lly me dog, he's,
me familiar. I mean you've got to decide
whether he's yer pet or the spawn o' Satan
now 'aven't ya—

But when I'm mixin' herbs he's underfoot
'cause he thinks it's gonna be chicken.
When me cauldron's boilin' he's stuck to me boot
'cause he thinks it's gonna be chicken.
When I'm carvin' chicken and dishin' it up
he thinks it's gonna be chicken which just goes to show,
if y' think somethin' long and hard enough,
if y' think it often and grand enough,
it'll make it true like a wizard can do.

Which is why I wanted to be a witch—a male witch—
so I can think things true,
without *raisin' the Wrath o' the Wizards*;
well they're not a very happy people
are they—whereas witches,
on the other 'and and not-with-standin',
are much cheerier than most people
think.

the desert station

I awake to jostling voices, the noise of arrivals, rise to walk the sleep out of bones. Hand over hand along the backs of seats, I avoid a tangle of robes and veils.

I hang out, cautiously, face to the hot wind over a rushing dark mass of rock and sand, left foot on the boarding step, right hand clinging white-knuckled to the steel handrail. The dusty night air is almost bearable, behind clamped lips and spare breath. But I can still taste the grit, and feel it piling up in my hair with each dry gust.

The train slows down. Bright lights ahead cast a powdery yellow against the lowering sky. A station looms, rises unassuming from a daguerreotype sea of robes, and a crowd ripples, swarms, and spills around the barrier. There are prayer-beads now, tossed and dangling over white cuffs. Dark eyes peer out above cloth dusted with the desert. Auburn fingers dipped in henna, ornately patterned, press black veils to invisible faces. Slender bodies move with grace in the sensuous flow of garments. Heavier ones move with stuffed authority, or not at all. Now I remember the dream:

—But how do you know if a woman is beautiful? Completely covered in black from head to toe. How can you tell, how can you tell?

—You look the hands, my teacher. If the hands are beautiful then she is all beautiful. And she know this, look, see the woman, there. See how she hang the limp-wristed. She is beautiful, and she want the man to know this.

—Very beautiful indeed. Sort of, stirring the air.

—Oh my teacher, she stir, believe me.

—Walla?

—Real-ly. Praise the God.

— Alhamdulillah.

time

Pine sentinels, loblolly stalks,
tufts of needles for a crown,
wear the sleek and gleaming dress
fashioned by a softly hammered
rataplan of rain and wind—
Broadleaf hands cling to a memory,
fiery age of oak and maple
clawing at the dark and velvet past.

Through weaves of once- and evergreen
warp and woof of nature's loom,
warm-lit windows summon medleys—
scented apple and cinnamon mornings,
sugared edges burnt and love-brushed
apron pockets filled with fancies,
winks beneath a candied rooftop,
old and young that dance to a mythic feast.

Town lights steam across the bay
plunging to the spectral depths
to build their mirrored towers aglow—
what of shadows, bones and memories,
light and song, will carve its outline
on the fossil slate, in tomorrow's mist?

hushed tales, hushed voices,
in the night of broken glass
Kristallnacht, 2000

Hushed tales
of ovens, line-ups pushed in,
darkness, where the heartbeat fails.
Selection now Satanic gesture; all these lessons
numbly nailed across the hearth, these cold confessions,
served as love and food regale our picnic
line-up, line-ups pushed in, tales
of ovens, coven tales.

Was it like the bad witch?
Not the good witch bags of spice and dreams,
but the bad apple witch with poison
fattening boys and girls—for the oven?
Was it like the bad witch?
Olga, Magda, Rózsikám,
bring the deviled eggs with kindness,
come and tell us what you saw,

spill the blood-red pàprika, yellow suns on emerald lawn,
spoon and spoon, spoon the memories
onto leafy greens, and china.
   No more now. The hand came down three times.
And I was spared. Three times I came, and the hand
came down for 'no more', three times was I spared.
   I carried my mother upon my back,
her ninety pounds and no life, barely skin
and the bone barely breath when they said,
'You Can Stay. We Will Help You'.
Lovely soldiers, the Americans.
So I thanked them, it was over but, oh no.
   No. Where's the child?
   Not one minute one more minute not one minute
will I spend—
   Rózsi, shhh—
   It was quiet. I remember.
No more sobbing silent sobbing,
no more barking hellish dogmen, they were gone.
And the gray sky found the blue, and the silence turned
to motors droning softly for the gift,
for the Manna-Fall from Heaven
   Chocolate fell. There was chocolate, all around,
children's dreams raining sweetly from the skies.
   Children's dreams—
   Was it like the bad witch?
   Shhh...

                                    And these trails
                        to slumber blind us, crushed in
                     darkness where the heartbeat rails
              at rejection, tortured manic pleasures all their evil
        crumbling, darkly tossed athwart the coldest measures
                             of love's lemonade, at Sunday picnic
                          line-up, line-ups pushed in, tales
                               of ovens, coven tales.

laughter

Nothing here for me now, caged in battle and pain,
seeking all the deep values of strife.
There's a child at the door to the welcoming school;
there's a spark that wants keeping alive.

I remember a land where the mountains were green,
simple elegance trellised in wood,
where a wineglass stood dappled in watery sun
that was native, and nurturing, and good.

Where a sweetwater lake harbored warm silhouettes
that were bound to a knowledge beyond;
and the trail to divinity danced among pines
to a place where laughter belonged.

chicago

Hog Butcher for the World...
Stormy, husky, brawling
City of the Big Shoulders: —*Carl Sandburg*

Hog Butcher Up And Left—
thought he'd leave the South Shore
to the metal-brewing poisonmakers—
KILL THAT WATER KILL IT DEAD!
'Course, any-yass-wipe fool along duh jungle stream
knows yoo doo not crap where you drink—
maybe dat's why duh Hog Butcher up 'n' left:
his shit was just, too, Organic.
Still...

They took that steel-shine, stacked it up and made it fly,
made you feel real proud just to get a kink in your neck
looking way up high past the Dow Jones,
right up to where the sky
she lay like drama,
over the Cloud Gate down below—
'on the ground,' where Soap-bubble Reality
fixes everything. Like that culture gap thing with
New Yawk, New Yawk

Child,
There is *never a night with nothin' to do in the Windy Cité*
There is *always something goin' down in town*
There is *something for and to oh-fend...*
Everybody.
'Sides, there's lotsa folks'd rather have
Half a Polish down by the Lake (that's the sausage)
than One Whole Russian at Coney Island (that's not)
DOBRZE, baby, *DOBRZE*.

I don't have no problem with that
Hog Butcher leaving though.
Stunk to high heaven: folks who had people to visit
up in Milwaukee— on the weekend? —
had no idea what we were talking about.
But on your way back home
from Indianapolis, Terre Haute,
Peoria and Points South, *DAMN!*—
You'd be sleeping in the back seat dreaming
Lake Shore Drive,
then your eyes would boomerang open, go
Hey... I must be home... (sniff) Love that organic waste!

And there was that Colombian *turista* once,
looked heavenly going *Chicágo-Chicágo, Al Capón, righ'?*

But *No,* said the undergraduate ingénue,
That's all cleaned up now, all over!
Yeah, all over City Hall.
But somebody had the *cojones*—*LOS COJONAZOS*—
To hold back a bunch of City Hall Salaries
till they finished doing their City Hall Jobs
Now that's *'My Kind of Town'*...

And I can still see those pictures of mama—
Mama who was Polish and Italian and African and Irish
and Jewish and Hungarian and Czech Off That List
I can still see them pictures—
she be-lookin like the Andrews Sisters,
wearing them shoulder pads that *held* up
a World War Two tailored suit,
dancing around with a flower in her hair
over at the Green Mill Lounge,
just down the street from the Aragon Ballroom,
which went and morphed into *El Aragón,*
somewhere between Perez Prado and Gay Pride—

But hey, if you're Italian,
*you can get your very own de-signer home
with no, windows, exposed, to the street,*
if you want, *if* U-R-I-talian. And if you're Jewish,
you can get your kid's bar mitzvah suit
from the Ghost of a Tailor down on Maxwell Street,
prob'ly get a double order of Maxwell Grilled Onions
stuffed in the breast pocket *if* you want, *if* you are Jewish,
and if you Black, *if* you are African American,
you can still get that *rib special,*
down on the SOUTH-side, down the basement?—
and that African Queen
be-layin on some Extra, Hot, Sauce,
whether or not you are African, American.

Because Something Happened Here—
right here where the Cold Wind blows—
Naw, it ain't cold. It's duh fric-kin Moon,
it's planet Pluto unfit for human habitation
when the Cold Wind blows—
Something Happened Here.
And it keeps right on happening.
And it looks kinda fine
tastes kinda sweet
sounds kinda hot
and it don't smell too bad neither
now 't that Hog Butcher up 'n' left.

But they tell me if you *hang-around down-around*
Forty-Second and Halsted,
you can still smell the yards.
Prob'ly some old sausagemaker working
down in the basement—
Or maybe the Indelible Shadows of Blood and Evil
lingering long past their prime—
Or maybe just the Spirit of Christmas Past,
helping Scrooge remember where it all comes from,
dragging a few *Smoky Links* behind.

60

style

They found a style in wartime clubs:
Big Bands, Big Headlines streaming out the door
through smoke and glass.

He wore a film-noir hat
that helped him
See Things Clearly.
She combed a white gardenia
to a jaunty peak just beyond her gaze,
and painted lips and nails to match
sweet passion's dream.

Their shoulder pads
could dance them to the floor.
He led. She followed. Followed well,
her backhand resting fingers Spanish-poised
against his pinstriped cloth they stepped,
and stepped, and stepped again,
as though they Owned
the right to scheme

                          their future?
                          Anyone's guess,
for style was all. It clung to them
through days and worlds without end.

And when their lives had run them down
to the Seven-Eleven for beer and chips,
she let her whiskers grow, and grow,
her own grey garden just to spite
that film-noir hat she almost loved
and would not live without.

meditation and dance

Stars reigning—beneath a cloudless sky—
were deities we've worshipped,
our former selves once loved.
The seed of Brahma—a gentle, fiery seed—
descended to a world lost
to Mother Sea, then instruments
arose—And the first to dance—
attired in princely raiment,
was Adi Dev, first deity,
first man—in love with womankind—
preserved in Vishnu's arms of love,
and to his dance there came
a sea of sisters—Kumaris, come to sing—
from high atop Mount Abu,
a truth that wanted song:
The redwood cone—to bear the mammoth tree—
must suffer the seed to dwell in fire
for the sapling's climb to heaven.
Thus souls that grow—from stunted seed
and nightmare—
through tempest walks and coaxing fires
will rise, and will become
stars reigning—beneath a cloudless sky—
deities we've worshipped,
our former selves now loved.

an american powwow

In the heartbeat of the drum, where sinews bind the dancer to the prayer, gratitude is a breath taken with every step, every leap that shoots an arrow to the sun. In the cadence of the Trot and of the Snake and Buffalo, the gathering in of Nations will embrace the tribes of Europe, and Africa, and all of humankind bound to Mother Earth, this fertile world. In the time between two harvests, given all we need, we come to understand our severed roots.

In this pride and place, where no one, nothing ever stands alone, family walks the Earth and Sky, for love of the Creator's knowing touch. Faith can dwell in comfort with us now, like elkskin pressed to music round the dreamer drum, like a love flute that sings to a lionheart knife. To make good use of dreams in the web of life, sinews bind the dancer to the prayer.

ABOUT THE AUTHOR

Cary Kamarat, a native of Chicago, received his MA from Northwestern University's School of Communication. He has taught at Evergreen State College in Washington State and NATO Defense College in Rome. He has also lived and worked in England, Spain, and Saudi Arabia. His poetry has been published in *The Federal Poet, District Lines Anthology, Prospectus,* online at *Poets on the Fringe* and *First People: Native American Poems and Prayers,* and has been aired on Israel National Radio. T*he Academic Exchange Quarterly* has published his teacher research, his photography has appeared in *The Tulane Review,* and he has reached a broad international audience through his travel blog at *www.travelwalk.blogspot.com.* He reads his own poetry regularly at several venues in the Washington DC area, and is now a resident of Maryland's Eastern Shore, where he takes a sailor's delight in the beauty of the Chesapeake.

Reviews

Travelwalk is a beautiful collection. I read it in one sitting, absorbing the lovely imagery and the accompanying photographs which fit perfectly with each poem. Cary has created a homage to the traveler in all of us, bringing the reader with him on his journey, making us taste, feel, and smell the multilayered experience that is travel and knowing a different place and time.
—Rosa Sophia, *Literary Editor, Member of the Editorial Freelancers Association*

In *Travelwalk: Poems and Images*, **Cary Kamarat** gives the reader a glimpse of the places he's lived and known and contemplated. In thoughtful style, his flowing passages paint a picture of the poet's mind regarding many facets of life in the places that could very well be any place, and open the mind to wondering and longing to learn and experience more of what life has to offer. A poet who can do this has indeed done his job.
—Matt Vossler, *Author and Book Industry Specialist, www.oaklightpublishing.com*

Cary Kamarat writes about a world where the busy thumbs of tweeters have replaced the caresses of lovers and the Barcelona beat fills that Dragon's Cave in the land of the Catalans. Traveling with this author's observant poems and images is always a pleasure.
—Prof. William Heath, *Mount Saint Mary's College, Author, Poet, Editor*

These lines pulse, shake and bounce. Perfectly matched with stunning photos, the words leap and summon the essence of each locale. Whoosh!
—Jason Brody, *Founder, Awakening Seminars.*

Kamarat's words and images journey to every continent, including the least known, the Self.
—Prof. Roser Caminals-Heath, *Hood College,*
Author and Translator

A solid piece of work. Cary Kamarat has a distinctive literary voice, a sense of economy, and an eye for memorable images.
—Jerry Bloom, *Actor and Voiceover Artist*

CPSIA information can be obtained
at www.ICGtesting.com
Printed in the USA
BVHW022134270321
603547BV00001B/3